My Beautiful BODY

Carly Rowena

ILLUSTRATED BY
Alf & Florence

Copyright 2021 by Carly Rowena | Published by Carly Rowena | Illustrations by Alf & Florence
ISBN: 978-1-7398125-3-9

All Rights reserved. No part of this publication may be reproduced, copied, stored in a retrieval system, or transmitted, in any form or by any means, without the prior written consent of the copyright holder, nor be otherwise circulated in any form of binding or cover other than that in which it is published and without a similar condition being imposed on the subsequent purchaser.

"Let us always be toddlers who strut with our bellies forward"

To Jax, always be you.

I found it

underneath

my clothes,

and in my wellies
where I wriggle my toes.

It loves to dance

and

<u>jump</u> and crawl,

And lets me grow from small to tall.

It loves to make noises that make me giggle,

I can

toot-toot

from my

butt-butt,

And snort when I sniffle.

It comes in all colours and sizes and shapes,

And loves to eat everything,

especially <u>cakes</u>.

We play with our food,

the bath and our toys,

And stomp like a dinosaur

and make lots of noise.

My beautiful body is my best friend to keep,

It never leaves me lonely

and is there while I sleep.

Together for adventures like <u>jumping</u> in puddles,

No matter what happens,

we'll always have cuddles.

My beautiful body,
my own little home,

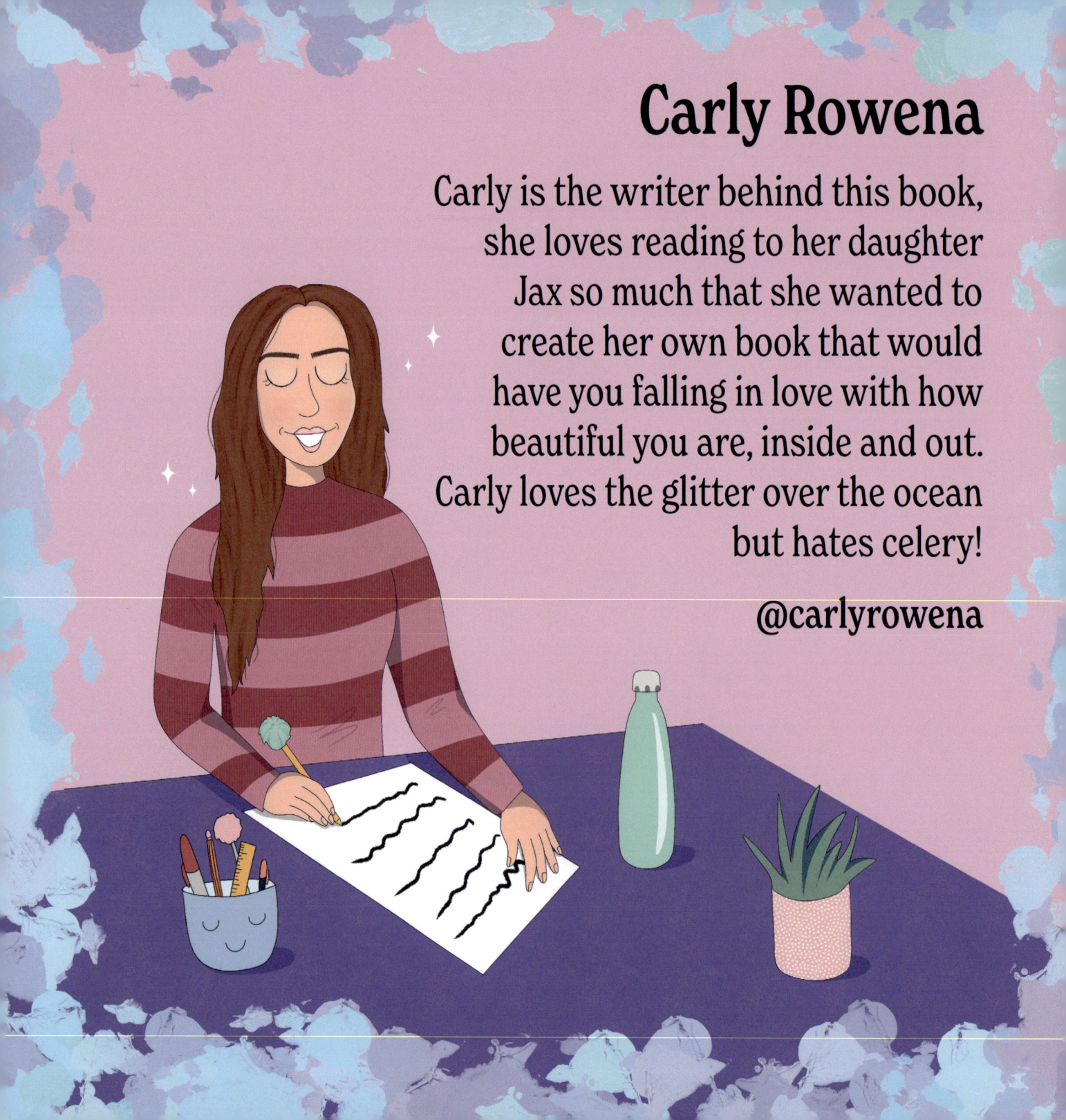

Alf & Florence

Alex Jones is the illustrator behind Alf & Florence and had so much fun drawing this book. She loves drawing self affirming happy illustrations of people and animals. She loves a warm bubble bath but hates spiders!

@alfandflorence

Printed in France by Amazon
Brétigny-sur-Orge, FR